A 30-DAY GUIDE TO YOUR

POWER

POWERFUL OUTCOMES
—— THROUGH ——
POWERFUL WORDS

IVETTE MAYO

Published in the United States of America
"A 30-Day Guide to Your Power: Powerful Outcomes Through Powerful Words."

Authored by: Ivette Mayo

Houston, Texas
Copyright © 2016 by Ivette Mayo

www.ivettemayo.com

Email Address: info@ivettemayo.com

Additional Websites: www.yosoyiam.com

www.ivettemayo.com

Irma~

always share

your power with

the World!

Curtis May

#POWERON

DEDICATION

This book is dedicated to the people that no matter what, love all of me -

To my Mami and Papi, my husband, Michael and our two amazing daughters, Leah and Danielle.

And to my new joy, Lola!

Anne Bengtson, thank you for inspiring me to teach.

CONTENTS

"A 30-Day Guide to Your Power"

Powerful Outcomes Through Powerful Words

Introduction *p.9*

INTRODUCTION

Know thyself. — Socrates

We all have our issues. We are all going to have our problems. We are going to have our obstacles. But there is one thing that you never want to do, and that is it to become a victim of your circumstances. You don't want to become a victim of your DNA. You don't want to become a victim of your environment. You have to take control of your own life. You have the opportunity to be all you can be POWERFULLY.

Everyone is propelled by their beliefs. There are religious beliefs, those of community, political, family and even beliefs about ourselves. A lot of those beliefs have been handed down and entrenched in all of us. These beliefs create a state of normalcy for us. We have been conditioned not to question them at the moment of transfer. We simply accept beliefs and continue on our journey; until we reach a cross-road in our life. Then, we begin to do one thing – SORT. We begin to question our beliefs. In some perverse way, we become uncomfortable and begin to be nonconforming. This is not necessarily bad. But, others may begin to view you as being difficult, unreasonable and even ungrateful. Why? You have played along all this time. Why did you stop playing along and enabling them to have their way now?

When I journeyed from my little town of Manati, Puerto Rico at the age of six with my family to my daddy's next duty station of Norfolk, Virginia, little did I know that it would begin a lifetime filled with change. I was always adapting to a new community, immersing myself into a new language, being exposed to new foods, people and music. But the constancies in my life were found within the confines of my home. Mami and Daddy were there to share culture and traditional mindsets from our island nation. I was the only daughter and how I was raised was different from the way my brothers were. I was introduced to a double standard at an early age. Women fulfilled a certain role in life, family and in marriage.

At twenty-one years of age, I found myself expecting my first child and marrying a professional athlete. In a short amount of time, I would be living in another state far from everything I knew. As we moved to different cities to play on different teams, I found comfort in my traditional upbringing and roles. My focus became serving my family and creating a home wherever we were. The challenge I faced throughout the marriage was; I was always making certain that everything was okay for everyone else. I went from being a dutiful daughter to a dutiful wife. As the twelve-year marriage began to break apart because of infidelity, verbal and mental abuse and then finally physical abuse; I struggled with this emotional life crisis. I found myself uncomfortable, doubtful and even down right unaccepting of inherited beliefs and social norms. I began to question even my spirituality. As I stood there at the ripe old age of thirty-three, doubt began to tear apart my foundation. Facing this life crisis and what I believed for years was betraying me.

"In life, there are some people you're going to have to lose in order to find yourself." - Unknown

I know I am not the only one that has experienced this sense of being lost. After seeing my marriage come to an end, facing the challenges of single motherhood, being a strong role model for my two beautiful daughters and a full-time job that required me to travel; I was being tested by experiencing profound loss. I came to the realization that I needed to get focused on breaking free. Up to this moment, I had enabled others. I participated in my life as a giver. Allowing others to have their way, I now needed to find my way. I needed to define my own self-truth. I was so blessed to have a real friend that witnessed my torment and circumstance firsthand. She called me over to her home. She handed me a blank check and said to me "There are several thousand dollars in this account. Use what you need to rid yourself of your pain. You deserve to have the life you want. Pay me back later, but don't stay where you are." Shocked by her generosity and words of encouragement, I accepted the blank check and went home. My reality had set in. The only thing keeping me from taking the needed next step was my beliefs. I believed what was holding me back from dealing with my situation was three things: I didn't have the money I needed to file for the divorce, I was scared and I didn't believe in myself. The check and my friend's words gave me power and more power than ever before. The money gave me the ability to make the decision I needed to make. My fear began to diminish. My belief in myself began to grow. I started to speak power into myself every day, "I AM Capable. I can do this!"

"You have the power to say, my story will not end this way."
- Unknown

Like a phoenix rising out of the ashes, I was able to rise POWERFULLY. I continue to speak my POWER to this day. I discovered the power to create the life I wanted rather than the one I had settled for. I came to realize that I already had considerably more power than I was are of, and the source of that power was already within me. I had the power of choice; I had given that power away too freely in the past. I now understand that the failure to choose or act proactively often leads to blaming someone else for the negative circumstances; rather than acknowledging your own role in the outcome.

After advancing two years, I found myself filled with joy. My daughters were flourishing. I had a great job and I loved every part of my life. As I began to build up strength and confidence, I decided that I also deserved to love again and be loved. I began to speak out loud of the kind of love I wanted and deserved. I spoke of the person I wanted as a partner, friend and lover. On August 24, 1997, I went on my first date in over fourteen years. His name was Michael Mayo, we met at work. It was a steamy Sunday afternoon in Houston. Over the jazz brunch menu, we talked about everything under the sun. He made me laugh and he drew me in with his intellect. The conversation went on for hours. We made it to a movie before ending our date. Before heading out, I looked back and said "I had a great time. I would love to go out again." He smiled back and said, "Me too." Mike and I were married exactly two years and four days later. We have been together ever since. He is perfect for me.

My ability to align my faith, gifts, talents and to speak my self-truth has become my internal compass – my TRUE North. It became my path to fulfilling my dreams. You can do so just by being yourself, and developing the gifts already inside you too. Can you recall a time when you felt intensely alive? A moment when you could say with confidence, "This is the real me?" That is when you are in sync with your True North. It is derived from your most deeply held beliefs, values, and the principles that lead you. It is your internal compass, unique to the POWERFUL you, representing who you are at your deepest level.

"I am not a victim of the things that happened to me. I choose to seek from deep within me to become who I desired to be – A POWERFUL ME!"

-Ivette Mayo

CHAPTER ONE

WHAT HAS POWER OVER ME?

"I am releasing that which has had power over me for far too long. I am taking my POWER back today."- Ivette Mayo

I often think of my grandmother when I would get in a situation that required me to keep moving forward and not get stuck. I can hear her hoarse voice saying in Spanish "Si tu quieres, tu puedes." (Translation "If you want to, you can do it.") Those words have given me POWER over the years to overcome many a situation. They reinforce me and build up my courage to continue to keep going forward in spite of my fear. God knows there were times I got so stuck that a stick of dynamite could not move me. Self-doubt and fear can paralyze a person. Those words given in love by my grandmother, decades ago, have become the match that lights the fuse for me. Regardless of the situation, I have found a way to continue. She didn't know it then, or did she? She was starting to condition me to not accept limiting beliefs, to encourage me to push past the fear and to speak power into myself. Most importantly, she wanted me to know that anything is possible if you desire it; regardless of what others may say or believe. As I begin to share my thoughts, feelings and processes with you, please recognize it comes from a place of growth and empathy. Like everyone else, I too have lived a complicated life filled with challenges, setbacks and great disappointments. Each one has deemed itself to be a teachable moment. It is a blessing to have lived through it and grown from it and then being able to impart that wisdom to others. Each lesson learned, good, bad or however ugly did not deter me from what I sought out. "Si tu quieres, tu puedes."

When confronted with a road block, you will figure a way around it. You must choose a strategy to win in order to achieve your goals with honor, integrity and joy. As I look around where I find myself right now, I am happy. I have been blessed abundantly. I have a wonderful husband and a forever partner in life. I have given life to fabulous daughters that I am so proud of. I have found a new kind of love through the smiles of my granddaughter. Over the course of my journey, I have experienced great travel adventures, amazing friendships and the ability to pursue my purpose to teach. I have started two successful companies and I know there is more to come. I have experienced grace and favor. I honor each gift because I know I have lived two lives in parallel. I say this, only to highlight, that we often employ our words to share the stories of what went wrong without showing appreciation for what did happen and for what we have and possess. I often say, "If I had to go through my life again to get where I am, I would do it all the same way." I have gained a great respect for the lessons life has taught me. I find comfort in sharing them now.

Like many people, we all have some moments in our lives that we all consider as life changing. They serve as triggers. They are usually an emotional event that rapidly sets off a chain reaction which causes us to respond. These life re-runs take you back to that place and time all over again. Your reaction can be physical, emotional or verbal. Heck, it can be all three responses at once. Your trigger can be set off by a smell, a song or even a word that resides in your emotional rolodex. When you experience it, it causes you to react without thinking, positively or negatively. Most auto-responses like this can cause stress and flashbacks; they can ruin relationships and careers. At the very least keep you from growing effectively. The good news is you have the power to over-ride them. You can choose how you respond to them to steer your

17

life clear in whatever direction you want. Once you shift your emotional state, you can examine if someone or something is actually taking something away from you or not. You no longer have to live your life based on some twenty-year-old memory that has a hold on you; sadly enough, it was placed upon you by someone else. You can work to let it go. Better yet, you can take control and move on.

One of my biggest personal triggers took place in November of 1995. I was in a challenging relationship. Over time, I allowed it to rob me of my voice. This moment felt like a large black cloud that covers the sun. I had to overcome the situation by choosing a positive outcome for myself. I chose me and I regained my voice. I regained my power. I promised myself that day and every day since, no one could silence me again.

Be sure to take these vital points away with you from our time together, that is to: *1.) ensure that you use words to elevate your state of mind 2.) increase your self-worth 3.) continue moving towards your purpose and 4.) to speak your* **POWER.**

Take a deep breath and close your eyes. For a few minutes, reflect on how you feel about what you are doing and where you find yourself right now? How do you feel about what you see? Open your eyes. What do you feel? Do you like what you're feeling one-hundred percent? It is time to make the decision to **SHIFT** your mind and everything around you from negative to positive, and free yourself from the judgment of others. Most importantly, to stop worrying about what others think about you altogether and to learn to distance yourself from disruptive judgement. Build the ability to remove negative thinking and negative messages, this will allow you to connect to innovative actions and fresh results. Once you have acquired these mechanisms, you will be able to smile at the world with a renewed sense of self and joy. I'm encouraging you to become the person you truly want to be.

Each role in my life has created responsibilities and behaviors like a daily road map. My roles as a daughter, mother, wife, friend, and employee made me re-focus my energy in performing these tasks to meet my obligations as expected. These expectations placed on me by others were hidden behind the cloak of traditional mindsets, culture, society and the structured job descriptions. These expectations required me to perform duties as needed not desired and were driven by the need to comply and conform. This is what was taught for generations. In my roles, I was successful. I wasn't "fulfilled." The success was not always accompanied by the feeling of joy. You know the kind of joy that is a source of intense pleasure or delight. The kind of joy that makes you smile like a child with a pocket full of change at an old-school candy store. The kind of joy that makes you dance in the grocery store.

As you move into this journey of transformational thinking, my desire is to help you to find your joy and that you no longer believe or care what others think or expect from you. Hopefully, you can begin to achieve new results because you are no longer fearful of taking necessary risks or tied to pleasing others. Most importantly, you no longer believe the lies that you have been told. For far too long, developing and accepting negative thoughts and messages, in all shapes and sizes, discouraged you from being proactive and hindered your ability to move forward. There is no better time than right now to stop playing this losing hand. Yes, stop giving these negative messages power over you. Because you see, I believe you can!

Negative limited thinking and messaging are your enemies. Recognizing this as your truth from this moment forward is the first step. It dampens your passion and motivation. It contributes to indecision, apathy, procrastination and outright derailment of your goal-directed actions. It holds you back and defeats you. It creates the "bad luck" that you will later regret. A major problem is, you are so used to these negative words and messaging that you aren't even aware when you are using them. You keep repeating those negative thoughts and words, inherited from others over time, so easily while continuing to give them life and importance. Therefore, you need to listen closely to the content of your words and thoughts. You need to hear your words as you speak them and recognize that they are negative and no longer serve you. You need to stop using them and replace them with more appropriate messages that are positive and optimistic, based on your real truth, not fear. This also will allow you to begin shaping your transformation when it comes to what you want to change about yourself and your future. Your WORDS have power. Begin to use your power to assemble a new foundation.

Your transformation is about you. It is about shattering the crazy spin cycle. Just because things haven't worked out in the past doesn't mean they never will. Just because people around you have weakened your view of yourself, doesn't mean that it is true. Just because you have been rejected and disappointed in the past, doesn't mean that this is your final chapter and the fate that you must resign yourselves to accept. Just because you have been plagued with perceived bad luck doesn't mean that this is the way it will always be. Are you ready to stop the madness?

You must accept that you are the master of your fate and ruler of your destiny. Are you ready to roll? On an unconscious level, you have allowed your negativity to become a defense mechanism, a protective device that if something bad should happen, you won't be blindsided and can explain it away. For example, you would say "This always happens to me." By saying this you are anticipating failure and you think you are softening the blow of failure and its setbacks. This is no longer an option.

You have to create new outcomes for yourself. Keep in mind, as we stay in this state of negativity and of anticipated bad luck and failure, you are actually creating more of the same now and in the future. You have accepted it as your personal norm. "It blocks the flow of positive energy and directs the Law of Attraction to attract negative effects and their consequences rather than positive outcomes. It reinforces our fear and insecurity, and it diminishes our confidence and faith in ourselves and our objectives," states *Walter E. Jacobson, M.D.*[1] It takes courage to really look inside yourself and ask the "spiritual you" what you want and what it is that's stopping you from achieving your dreams. Is it the fear of failure, fear of success, lack of focus, childhood issues, not being good enough or is it something hidden deep within? On this journey of transformation, you must want to feel whole and complete. You have to prepare to add passion and belief in yourself deep in your soul. So, you can continue to move forward to your place of fulfillment. You want to stop being stopped. It is time to catapult yourself to another level of growth and joy. We can find ourselves stuck on a job that we don't like, giving half efforts while wishing and dreaming about something else daily. We have lost sight of our life's purpose and constantly feeling like we are spinning in circles; without truly accomplishing anything significant. It is time to regain control, be encouraged and create a new-found hope that will deliver new courage leading you to new action. You will have to learn to take on risks. Even if this means letting go of things you have found comfort in and accept that once you have committed to your goals and dreams, the magic will happen. I will not sugarcoat this for you. The need to stretch beyond those common places will be necessary. Especially if you want to free yourself from negative and limiting beliefs and to accept that you do deserve all that you dream of for yourself!

CHAPTER TWO

STEP INTO YOUR POWER

"Step into your power by developing the framework for your success." -Ivette Mayo

In order to change the decades of negativity, there has to be a desire to discard old processes to swap out your thoughts and emotions about yourself with brand new ones. It may seem like you are being asked to do something really difficult, but I am here to say, "You can do this with ease." I will walk you through crucial steps for your transformation. Each step will help you develop the framework for your success.

From your perception of the inner you, you will begin to notice this language emerging from a familiar voice which guides you. This development leads to the inner layers of yourself which are beginning to unfold. This unfolding is the process which leads you to a deeper relationship and understanding of self. Remember this relationship you have with yourself is directly in line with your relationship to partners, family, friends, coworkers, community and the world around you.

Conduct a Personal S.W.O.T. Analysis

Self-awareness improves your judgment and helps you identify opportunities for professional development and personal growth. By just taking a little time to identify areas in your personal and professional life, this will lead to achieving the fulfillment that you seek. You will no longer concede to the will of others. This is where you, by taking a Personal S.W.O.T. Analysis of yourself, will be helpful in your transformation. In business, you would not hesitate in conducting a S.W.O.T. Analysis to create a business plan and identify tactical strategies to achieve success, but we fail to do this in our personal lives. What a Personal S.W.O.T. Analysis helps you do is to identify your strengths and weaknesses, and analyze the opportunities and threats that flow from them. This is a helpful technique that will benefit you.

What makes a Personal S.W.O.T. Analysis especially powerful is that, with a little time and thought, it can help you uncover opportunities that you would not otherwise have spotted. By understanding your weaknesses, you can manage and eliminate threats that might otherwise hurt your ability to move forward. If you look at yourself using the S.W.O.T. framework, you can start to separate yourself from your past and your challenges. The S.W.O.T. framework highlights the specialized talents and skills you need to advance your career and help you achieve your personal goals and dreams and it will help you to step into your POWER. Here is the S.W.O.T. framework and its components; Strengths, Weaknesses, Opportunities and Threats. (Personal S.W.O.T. Analysis by Mindtools, www.mindtools.com)[2]

Strengths

- What do you do well?
- What unique resources can you access?
- What advantages do you have that others don't have? (for example, skills, certifications, education, or connections)
- Which of your achievements are you most proud of ?
- What values do you believe in that others fail to exhibit?
- Are you part of a network that no one else is involved in? If so, what connections do you have with influential people?

If you have any difficulty identifying your strengths, write down a list of your personal characteristics.

Weaknesses

- What could you improve?
- Where do you have fewer resources than others?
- What tasks do you usually avoid because you don't feel confident in doing them?
- What will the people around you see as your weaknesses?
- Are you completely confident in your education and skills training? If not, where are you the weakest?
- What are your negative work habits? (for example, are you often late, are you disorganized, do you have a short temper, or are you poor at handling stress)
- Do you have personality traits that hold you back in your field? For instance, if you have to conduct meetings on a regular basis, a fear of public speaking would be a major weakness.
- Consider this from a personal/internal perspective and an external perspective. Do other people see weaknesses that you don't see? Be realistic. It's best to face any unpleasant truths as soon as possible. Your goal is to minimize or eliminate these weaknesses.

Opportunities

- What opportunities are open to you?
- What trends could you take advantage of ?
- How can you turn your strengths into opportunities?
- Is your industry growing? If so, how can you take advantage of the current market?
- Do you have a network of strategic contacts or mentors to help you or offer good advice? Who are they?
- Take a moment to look at your strengths, and ask yourself what opportunities do my strengths open up for me? then look at your weaknesses, and ask yourself whether you could create opportunities by eliminating those weaknesses?

Threats

- What threats could harm you?
- What is your competition doing?
- What threats do your weaknesses pose to you?
- What obstacles do you currently face at work or at home?
- Are the demands for your skills and on your job changing?
- Could any of your weaknesses lead to threats?

- Performing this analysis will often provide key information. It can point out what needs to be done and put challenges into perspective.

Use the chart below to write down your very own S.W.O.T. Analysis framework. Use this information to build your **POWER.**

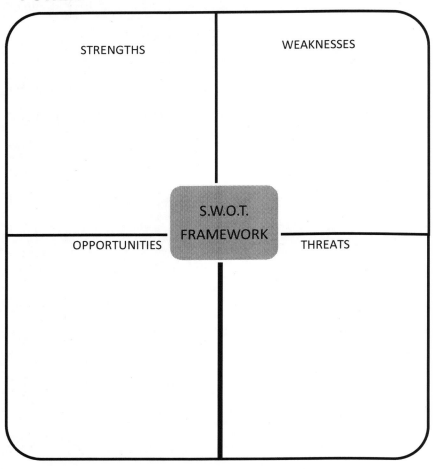

CHAPTER THREE

THE POWER OF SELF AWARENESS

"To become more self-aware, you should develop a deeper understanding of yourself in multiple areas." -Ivette Mayo

Sometime back, I came across a book that laid things out for me in regards to my self-awareness, "*Making the Most of Your Talents - Opportunities Self-Awareness and Personal Development", by Dr. Scott Williams* [3]. What stood out for me was the need for me to develop an understanding on what drives me and why. We all struggle with that at times. Each day it is highlighted by the chaos around us. It turns into noise. Developing filters to remove or minimize the chaos and noise will serve you well.

Key Areas for Self-Awareness

Human beings are complex and diverse. To become more self-aware, you should develop an understanding of yourself in multiple areas. Key areas for self-awareness include our personality traits, personal values, habits, emotions, and the psychological needs that drive our behaviors. It is important for you to identify what really drives you.

Personality

We don't normally change our personalities, values and needs based on what we learn about ourselves. But, an understanding of your personality can help you find situations in which you will thrive, and help you avoid situations in which you will experience the most stress. For instance, if you are a highly-introverted person, you are likely to experience stress when speaking in public than a highly-extroverted person would. So, if you are highly introverted, you should either learn skills to cope with the demands of speaking in public that requires extravert-type behavior patterns, or you should find a position that is more compatible with your personality.

Values

It's important that we each know and focus on our personal values. For instance, if your first priority is "being there for your children" or "your relationship with God," it's very easy to lose sight of those priorities on a day-to-day, moment-by-moment basis. During the workday, so many problems and opportunities arise that our list of "things to do" can easily exceed the time you have to do them. Since few of those things pertain to what you value most, it's easy to spend too much time on lower priority activities. When you focus on your values, you are more likely to accomplish what you desire.

Habits

Our habits are the behaviors that we repeat routinely and often automatically. Although you would like to possess the habits that help you interact effectively with and manage others, we can probably all identify at least one of our habits that decrease our effectiveness. For example, creating a personal agenda prior to a meeting, that habit interfered with my ability to stay focused on critical ideas and to build team members commitment to the decisions at hand. This habit delayed progress and affected my ability to influence. Writing things down prior to meeting is now something I do every time.

Needs

Researchers have identified a variety of psychological needs that drive our behaviors such as needs for approval, affection, belongingness, achievement, self-actualization, power and control. One of the advantages of knowing which needs exert the strongest influence on your own behaviors is the ability to understand how they affect our interpersonal relationships. For instance, most of us have probably known people who have a high need for status. They seek high status positions within organizations. Such people also want titles that symbolize their status. They insist that they be shown respect and privileges. Needs cause motivation and when needs aren't satisfied; they can cause frustration, conflict and stress.

Emotions

Emotional self-awareness has become a hot topic of discussion; recently because, it's one of the five facets of emotional intelligence. Understanding your own feelings, what causes them, and how they impact your thoughts and actions is emotional self-awareness. If you were once excited about your job but not excited now, can you get excited again? To answer that question, it helps to understand the internal processes associated with getting excited. That sounds easier than it is. Here's an analogy, I think I know how my car starts. I put gas in the tank, put the key in the ignition and turn the key. But, my mechanic knows a lot more about what's involved in getting my car started than I do. He knows what happens under the hood. My mechanic is able to start my car on the occasions when I'm not because, he understands the internal processes. Similarly, a person with high emotional self-awareness understands the internal process associated with emotional experiences; therefore, has greater control over them.

CHAPTER FOUR

THE

POWER

RITUAL©

I am not happy. I am not fulfilled.

I procrastinate all the time too, but that is what I feel.

I don't know what I want anymore, for far too long I have allowed others to tell me what I need to do, how and when to do it.

But that stops today!

For I no longer accept unfulfillment and disappointment as my norm.

I have dreams and desires that will be realized!

Today, you will take steps in starting each day differently with "A 30 Day Guide to Your POWER". For the next thirty days, you will begin each day with a POWER RITUAL. A POWER RITUAL is about you stating what you want to accomplish and why. It will become a vital part of your transformation. Your words hold the key to what you want to achieve and desire when it comes to your personal success!

Nothing more – nothing less!

You have "perceived an inner truth" about yourself. Remember, your norms were beliefs that you have heard, done and believed about yourself for far too long. I want to move you past all of that, help you to stay focused on where you want to go and to move you to your next best level; a place of renewed energy, growth, unlimited opportunities and emotional stability.

It is time to CHANGE your NORMS to BECOME ANEW! Change Inner Truths or Beliefs.

Your beliefs are learned thought patterns that you have developed since childhood. Many of these do work well for you, but others may now be working against you. They can be dysfunctional and they may be sabotaging you from achieving what you want and believe.

"You have unlimited POWER!"

The **POWER RITUAL** will break the cycle that is keeping you from your place of personal strength. You can do anything you want. You can be anything you desire. You have to believe you can do it. The POWER Ritual's sole purpose is to create new, positive, and purposeful thoughts and beliefs in you. Simply by guiding you to change your words to generate more **POWERFUL** outcomes! Through the POWER Ritual you are aligning your words to create the "GREATEST I" ever – the I is YOU!

How can your words change the way you think, feel and react to events in your life?

You learn as you grow to interact with the world. You also create results based on your words; most importantly, how you feel and think. By making a conscious effort to change how you feel and think this will assist you in creating the powerful outcomes you desire.

You have the power to change your feelings and thoughts about yourself!

i-ffirmation© – creating daily self-focused positive statements fixated on what you want to **change**.

i-ffirmations are effective and useful. By creating and using i-ffirmations, you are making a choice about yourself. You are making yourself a priority. Every thought you think, every word you say is an **i-ffirmation.** All of our self-talk or inner dialogue is streaming from an **i-ffirmation**. You are continually supporting your state of being, subconsciously, with your words and thoughts. Your thoughts form the words that you speak giving your words the power to create into existence that reality. There are some important things to remember as you develop your daily **i-ffirmation**, in order to control your thoughts, you have to replace limiting beliefs to reprogram your subconscious of past negativities. Also, you need to have an emotional connection to fully want to change your speech. To affirm anything is to state it as if it is so and to maintain this as being true in the face of all evidence to the contrary.

By creating a positive flow of words or i-ffirmation, you are creating a NEW life experience - every day! Remember, what you can conceive, you can achieve!

Your Daily Tools

i-ttitude© - it starts with a statement of self-praise.

i-ttitude is a statement that protects your self-worth, personal values and desires for personal growth. It is a commitment to you. You are your own biggest critic and the co-creator of your own life. With that freedom, you have the immense power to decide who you are and who you would like to become. It gives you the ability to be a bit selfish. This is an opportunity to stretch and be uncomfortable because you were taught to be selfless and to always put others needs first. I want to remind you that this is why we are here now. You have placed

40

everyone and everything ahead of you. You can still have a servant's heart which allows for caring and giving to others. I am just asking you to make yourself a priority too. If you would like to see real change in your life, as well as success in your endeavors, you must learn to re-program your thoughts and keep them positive; especially the thoughts about yourself! As the co-creator of your reality, you have got to believe it to see it – that's why an "I AM" statement is so important.

i-ffirmations and i-ttitude always start with the two most POWERFUL words "I AM".

Examples of **i-ttitude**

I AM Deserving
I AM Successful
I AM Capable
I AM Loving

Let's allow the process to unfold through your daily creating.

I want to encourage you to really pledge real effort towards a POWERFUL You by beginning **Your POWER** Ritual. **It is time to distance yourself from negative thoughts and messages;** all negative thinking is fear-based. **The success of your transformation requires consistent**

effort. Your POWER Ritual is simply a way for you to challenge yourself to consistently create your new real truth by writing out and speaking a new i-ffirmation daily. Using i-ffirmations will become a daily assault on your past negative thinking and messaging. It will begin to reduce the affect and hold they have on you by replacing them with your NEW positive truth.

3 Steps to Change

The following steps are going to help you on your journey of transformation and allow you to remove negative thoughts and messages from your life. It is simply about letting go and aspiring to diminish the affects your past limited thoughts and negative messaging that exist in your life; and replace them with positive i-ffirmations and i-ttitude.

Step 1 Start with Awareness

The very first step of managing your negative thoughts is awareness. You must recognize that these thoughts and messages simply exist. Not only are they ever-present, they drive your behaviors and beliefs. They are on automatic. They pop up and take over.

Previously, in the Personal S.W.O.T. Analysis you were able to identify areas of strength, weakness, opportunities and threats. Use this information to form your i-ttitude and create focused i-ffirmations.

Step 2 Replace the Emotions! Let them GO!

When negative thoughts hit your brain over and over again, you accept them as your truth. Plain and simple. You have heard it all for so long that you don't allow yourself to believe anything else. But what you have failed to recognize is that it's not true at all. It is someone deflecting from their own shortsightedness onto you. Even when you wrestle with these negative thoughts and try to replace them with more positive thoughts it doesn't always work. Your emotions are attached to these negative thoughts. For the best results, try to imagine yourself emotionally "letting go". The "emotional let go approach" is used in yoga and meditation to help a person stay focused in the present moment.

I want to challenge you to stop replaying "bad" events and experiences in your head all they do is press the "re-live" button that allows all those emotions into the present. You cannot remove that experience from your life, but you can change how you deal with them and how you continue to "feel" about yourself.

This action is way over due and stop allowing this to dictate your life's outcomes. Turn off the "re-live" button. This will be extremely instrumental in helping you to shift your emotional space away from anger and hurt to forgiveness and self-love. The victim mentally cannot become an emotional ball and chain anymore. See yourself as a survivor and replace your ball and chain with a tall stage and tell your story of survival.

Step 3   Reinvent and Commit

It is important to be committed in body, mind and spirit to your transformation. You are going to begin tackling decades of negative programing. Deep rooted beliefs aren't going to melt away in one day. The process will require a daily assault on these past triggers. You are essentially made up of your habits and beliefs. Most people don't know that it takes at least twenty-one days to create a habit, and most of us haven't consciously created the habits we currently have. You inherit habits and beliefs from your parents and peers at an early age. But, what if you could consciously create new habits to transform your life?

You are what you repeatedly do every day – your rituals. Let the POWER Ritual begin. It will require that you begin to create new habits to reach your ultimate vision. Setting time aside for self-reflection and positive messaging is now necessary to have the success and happiness you want. You will need to set a time and place where it is quiet for your POWER Ritual. It may require that you get up a little early every day before the house begins to stir. It may feel uncomfortable at first but understand the results are worth pursuing. When things become uncomfortable it is because you are growing and change is taking place.

I want to encourage you to really pledge real effort towards a POWERFUL You by beginning Your POWER Ritual. It is time to distance yourself from negative thoughts and messages. All negative thinking is fear-based. The success of your transformation requires consistent effort. Your POWER Ritual is simply a way for you to challenge yourself to consistently create your new real truth by writing out and speaking a new i-ffirmation daily. Using i-ffirmations, will become a daily assault on past negative thinking and messaging. It will begin to reduce the hold they have on you by replacing them with your NEW positive truth.

The time is now for you to rid yourself of old habits. Get unstuck from those old thoughts and messaging. They have crippled you, paralyzed you, caused suffering and kept you trapped instead of allowing you to move forward towards a happier and more positive life. Let i-ffirmations create new outcomes in your life every day. Little by little you will begin to see the past become less significant and a new more powerful you arise.

"The world we have created is a product of our thinking; it cannot be changed without changing our thinking." -Albert Einstein

CHAPTER FIVE

POWER RESET: POWER RITUAL BEGINS

"The radical changes you desire requires your commitment to consistently apply this POWER RITUAL to your life."-Ivette Mayo

There is that word again – consistently. Here is the objective of the POWER RITUAL, we will aim to transform your personal thoughts and messaging with i-ffirmations to achieve a new i-ttitude. I want to challenge you to start your 30-Day POWER Ritual as soon as possible. It will stir up your courage and connect you to your POWER. Your POWER will begin to radiate a calm inner strength, inspiration and success in every part of your life.

Let me ask you some important questions:

- What is something you have heard about yourself all your life that you are tired of defending?
- What is something that you want to change in your life?
- What are you unhappy with?
- Why are you unhappy?
- What is something you'd like to add to your life that would enhance it?

These questions may apply to different areas in your life such as:

- health
- wealth
- relationships
- character

Your answers will bring to light areas that you can begin to focus on first.

As you begin Your POWER Ritual, I would like to suggest that you commit to using this journal for your POWER Ritual. Here you will capture your thoughts and feelings. It will serve as a great place for reflections. Each day you will state a new i-ffirmation for each new day.

Let's get started on the 4 easy steps:

Step 1 Start by writing DAY 1 at the top Left hand corner of the page.

Below the date, write your i-ffirmation for that day starting with "I AM"

Here is an example "I AM Deserving."

Step 2 State the POWER Mantra©

"I am committed to changing myself and removing the difficulties and challenges from my past and present life to create a happier and more POWERFUL Me. I desire to become better, feel better, and do better when it comes to me. I am releasing myself of a past that no longer suits me and embrace my gifts and my POWERFUL purpose." (The Power Mantra, Ivette Mayo[4])

Step 3 Re-state your i-ffirmation. I AM Deserving because…Continue writing down and capturing all the things that come to mind why you are deserving, plus things you want to achieve because you are deserving. Try not to judge what you are capturing on the page. Simply honor your spirit and emotions in the moment or state. Allow the statement to take shape without a critical eye. Don't sensor your heart. In the last sentence, you will restate your i-ffirmation – I AM DESERVING!

Step 4 Once your page is complete, you will now say your i-ffirmation out loud. Your i-ffirmation will need to take flight and allow you to hear your own words. These expressions of your heart's desire will now have life. By hearing it, you will start to believe it. You will begin to remember this moment and will continue to hear it over and over again in your head throughout the day.

Your new self-messaging or i-ffirmation will start to take hold and you will start to sense the change in your i-ttitude. You will begin to want to protect that feeling of self-worth. And you will honor it.

The POWER Ritual will begin to take flight. You ask what does this all mean? It means that by changing your personal words (or messaging about yourself), you will change your thoughts, your emotions, your actions and most importantly your outcomes. Those old triggers will no longer have the same effect on you. Those inherited thoughts about you are no longer your truth. You have created a new truth about yourself that truly and authentically represents you. Connecting you to the POWER you desire to achieve. This will become an expected part of your day.

It is time to TURN up the POWER!

CHAPTER SIX

30 DAY

JOURNAL

OF

I-FFIRMATIONS

THE POWER MANTRA

"I am committed to changing myself and removing the difficulties and challenges from my past and present life to create a happier and more POWERFUL Me. I desire to become better, feel better, and do better when it comes to me. I am releasing myself of a past that no longer suits me and embrace my gifts and my POWERFUL purpose."

-Ivette Mayo

TODAY'S I-FFIRMATION

Day_____

I AM DETERMINED

I AM DETERMINED, because I can accomplish anything I set my mind to. Every day, I take action to get closer to my goals. I AM DETERMINED, for I have learned to press on until the goal is reached. Each day, I AM overcoming obstacles and staying away from things that distract me from what is important. I AM DETERMINED, to keep those things that are negative and not for me, far from me. I AM proud of myself for having this spirited resolve to move towards my desires with confidence and DETERMINATION. I AM thankful for developing a strong, unwavering, personal DETERMINATION that makes me a priority! I face each new day as a race to be won. I AM strong enough to overcome anything.

I AM DETERMINED!

_____
_____
_____
_____
_____
_____
_____
_____
_____
_____
_____
_____

TODAY'S I-FFIRMATION

Day_____

I AM THANKFUL

At the beginning of every day, I count my blessings and give thanks for all that I have and all that I AM! I AM THANKFUL! At the end of each day; I take a moment to reflect on what happened to me and all I was able to accomplish. I AM THANKFUL! By being THANKFUL for what I have, brings more abundance into my life. Every day, I AM becoming more and more THANKFUL! Every day, I appreciate my life more and more. Every day, I AM THANKFUL for blessings seen and unseen. Every day, I AM THANKFUL for the universe for guiding me closer to my dreams. Every day I AM THANKFUL for the qualities and talents that make me so unique. Good things come to me because I AM THANKFUL.

I AM THANKFUL!

_____
_____
_____
_____
_____
_____
_____
_____
_____
_____
_____
_____

TODAY'S I-FFIRMATION

Day_____

I AM A GIVER

I AM A GIVER for I seek opportunities to reinforce others to empower and strengthen them. I AM A GIVER to help build up their confidence, resulting in better performance and to increase their personal happiness! I AM A GIVER for I have a SERVANT HEART. By giving to others small tokens of love and appreciation with my words and smiles, make me better! I AM A GIVER for I know by elevating others, I AM sharing my spirit!

I AM A GIVER!

_____
_____
_____
_____
_____
_____
_____
_____
_____
_____
_____
_____
_____
_____
_____
_____
_____

TODAY'S I-FFIRMATION

Day_____

I AM PROUD OF ME

I AM PROUD OF ME! As each day passes, I become more determined and committed to creating a better me. I AM breathing. I AM alive. I AM experiencing this moment meant for me. I release all my worry's and all thoughts of my past. They no longer hold me back. I AM here at this very spot enjoying all that surrounds me. I AM PROUD OF ME for what I have accomplished, survived and endured. I don't show my scars, but share experiences that have taught me that I AM a TRUE Warrior. I have courage, strength and persistence. I AM PROUD OF ME because I have HOPE for my future. I AM FAITHFUL. I have dreams that I know I can realize! I know myself, my gifts, and my talents. I AM happy and working each day to create stability around me. I AM PROUD OF ME! I AM looking upward to the highest star and I can see me SOAR!

I AM PROUD OF ME!

_____
_____
_____
_____
_____
_____
_____
_____
_____
_____

TODAY'S I-FFIRMATION

Day_____

I AM EXPECTING

I AM EXPECTING the things that I have sought for myself, my family and all those that I love! I AM EXPECTING the plan that I lay out will work throughout the year. I AM EXPECTING that every strategy and task is SUCCESSFUL and ACCOMPLISHES my desired outcome. I AM EXPECTING everything thing that I've learned and will learn, I will be able to implement with ease. I AM EXPECTING to gain influence and the support of others that can help pave my path to NEW HEIGHTS. I AM EXPECTING the RESOURCES I need to come to me quickly and abundantly. I AM EXPECTING RICHNESS in my life, for this is my season for GREATNESS! I AM EXPECTING LOVE so profound and true. I AM EXPECTING FRIENDSHIPS that are authentic and enduring. I AM EXPECTING great discernment on my part on WHAT and WHO I allow in my life. I AM EXPECTING that my eyes will see the blessings and gifts I have been given. Most importantly, I AM EXPECTING to put them to work for the good of others. I BELEIVE IT and CLAIM IT!

I AM EXPECTING!

_____
_____
_____
_____
_____
_____
_____

TODAY'S I-FFIRMATION

Day_____

I AM A DIAMOND

I AM A DIAMOND. I have been created under extreme temperatures and pressure. You may not see my imperfections, they lie deep below the surface. They do not define me, but rather inspire me. The things that are inside of me have no effect on my beauty or brilliance. Each element that I have endured has made me distinctive in color, size, and blemishes. I have handled PRESSURE exceptionally well. I AM UNIQUE, BEAUTIFUL and PRICELESS! Each day I CHOOSE to SHINE BRIGHTLY!

I AM A DIAMOND!

_____
_____
_____
_____
_____
_____
_____
_____
_____
_____
_____
_____
_____
_____
_____
_____
_____

TODAY'S I-FFIRMATION

Day_____

I AM TENACIOUS

I AM TENACIOUS! I AM unshakable when it comes to my dreams and goals! I AM persistent and focused on what I want to achieve! I AM stubborn and inflexible when it comes to what I want for me and my family! I AM TENACIOUS! Tenacious because for far too long I have put me aside. I AM TENACIOUS because I have created a plan for my success and I will not waiver. Being tenacious pays-off because what drives me comes from a place deep in my spirit. My personal drive and desire is the strong force that galvanizes my steadfast commitment to all that is important to me, my family, my career and my purpose!

I AM TENACIOUS!

_____
_____
_____
_____
_____
_____
_____
_____
_____
_____
_____
_____
_____
_____
_____

TODAY'S I-FFIRMATION

Day_____

I AM LOVED

I AM LOVED. I give love. When I give love, I will get love. Before I can give love, I will have to first love me! I AM LOVED and I constantly attract amazing people into my life who mirror my values, dreams, commitments and desires. My heart is always open and I radiate love. I AM LOVED and all my relationships are long lasting and loving. I see everything with loving eyes and I love everything I see. I deserve love and I get it in abundance. I love myself and everybody else and in return everybody loves me. I AM LOVED! Everywhere I go, I find love. Life is joyous.

I AM LOVED!

_____
_____
_____
_____
_____
_____
_____
_____
_____
_____
_____
_____
_____
_____

TODAY'S AFFIRMATION

Day_____

I CHOOSE PEACE

I CHOOSE PEACE. I feel grateful for all the abundance that flows into my life. PEACE comes when I let go of trying to control every tiny detail. I CHOOSE PEACE. I AM filled and surrounded with positive energy. I encourage PEACE in all my interactions with others. I give and receive PEACE and love gracefully and easily. I AM at PEACE within myself.

I CHOOSE PEACE!

_____
_____
_____
_____
_____
_____
_____
_____
_____
_____
_____
_____
_____
_____
_____
_____
_____

TODAY'S I-FFIRMATION

Day_____

I AM REAWAKENING

I AM REAWAKENING! My soul has a remembrance of its true power and nature. I rededicate myself to my highest purpose, whether spoken or not. I AM READY to continue! I see the possibilities of things that will allow me to grow, to take flight and to soar. I AM REAWAKENING. I will do away with the limiting thoughts, shatter fear and believe in the new beginnings to come.

I AM REAWAKENING!

_____
_____
_____
_____
_____
_____
_____
_____
_____
_____
_____
_____
_____
_____
_____
_____

TODAY'S I-FFIRMATION

Day_____

I AM FRUITFUL

I have been planting seeds for a long time. I have been and continue to work hard towards my goal and my dream. I AM FRUITFUL! I find myself in this hectic state of activities; I realize that I AM HARVESTING my harvest. It is so important not to let one opportunity be wasted. I AM FRUITFUL! All the things that I AM working on are the fruits of my labor. I AM living a life that is FRUITFUL!

I AM FRUITFUL!

_____
_____
_____
_____
_____
_____
_____
_____
_____
_____
_____
_____
_____
_____
_____
_____

TODAY'S I-FFIRMATION

Day_____

I AM CHOOSING

I have the ability to CHOOSE. I AM CHOOSING what is best for me! Far too many times I relinquish my POWER of CHOICE by deferring it to others or just letting FEAR creep in. I will CHOOSE what I WANT and NEED! I have to be fully committed to my desires, dreams and decisions each and every day. All my choices are in line with my desires. I CHOOSE my life, my goals and my dreams. Each decision I make presents amazing new possibilities for me. Every day, I have the option to make choices that support my well-being. Every moment of my life is full of choices. I AM ready to CHOOSE bolder options. I always have the freedom to CHOOSE. I AM going to experience it BOLDLY and FREELESSLY. I AM going to always use my POWER to CHOOSE...for ME!

I AM CHOOSING!

_____
_____
_____
_____
_____
_____
_____
_____
_____
_____
_____

TODAY'S I-FFIRMATION

Day_____

I AM PROTECTED

I embrace the new and unknown with the certainty that I AM always PROTECTED. I know I AM guided in the direction which is best for me. With my faith in God and all my gifts, I know how to navigate this new path which is filled with peace, happiness and hope. I AM not afraid to travel NEW ROADS! I AM PROTECTED! Everything in my path is to create increase and abundance in my life, in all that I do and all that I desire.

I AM PROTECTED!

_____
_____
_____
_____
_____
_____
_____
_____
_____
_____
_____
_____
_____
_____
_____
_____
_____
_____

TODAY'S I-FFIRMATION

Day_____

I AM TRANSCENDING

I have the courage and confidence that my DREAM is worth pursuing. I AM TRANSCENDING! I AM investing in me and finding the skills I need to better myself. I AM TRANSCENDING! I AM using my distinctive gifts every day to achieve my purpose. As I TRANSCEND, I AM moving to my next level. As I TRANSCEND, I AM willing to learn new things, do things differently and explore new possibilities.

I AM TRANSCENDING!

_____
_____
_____
_____
_____
_____
_____
_____
_____
_____
_____
_____
_____
_____
_____
_____
_____
_____
_____

TODAY'S AFFIRMATION

Day_____

I AM PRODUCTIVE

May all my meetings go smoothly today. All my work projects are ahead of schedule. All of my appointments are successful. Every day I accomplish more things in less time. I AM generating lasting wealth. I always approach my work by thinking of ways I can improve. I always arrive at my appointments with time to spare. I AM finding and signing new clients. I always deliver more than is expected of me. I AM a MASTER at what I do. I AM VERSATILE. I AM RESOURCEFUL.

I AM PRODUCTIVE!

_____
_____
_____
_____
_____
_____
_____
_____
_____
_____
_____
_____
_____
_____
_____
_____
_____
_____

TODAY'S I-FFIRMATION

Day_____

I AM GOOD

I AM in a place that I feel amazing! I AM in a place that I have purpose! I AM in a place that I have forgiven! I AM in a place that I AM full of energy. I AM in a place where I love what surrounds me. I AM in a place where I AM loved! I AM in a place that I AM getting healthier by the moment! I AM in a place that I have encircled myself with trusted mentors and friends. I AM in a place that my business is growing and momentum is building. I AM in a place that my hard work is paying off. I AM in a place that I can help others. I AM in a place that my faith in God continues to direct me and gives me clarity.

I AM GOOD!

_____
_____
_____
_____
_____
_____
_____
_____
_____
_____
_____
_____
_____
_____
_____

TODAY'S I-FFIRMATION

Day_____

I AM A LEADER

I cannot lead others if I AM not willing to lead myself. My GROWTH and SUCCESS is rooted in me. Every day I AM purposely seeking out knowledge and new experiences. Every day I AM working on directing myself to a position of strength and influence. I AM A LEADER. I pray for courage and boldness to take on new tasks and risks. I seek out people that can mentor me to gaining new insights. I AM A LEADER for I AM always building skills to grow. I AM A LEADER for I embrace responsibility. I AM A LEADER because I AM willing to teach others, desire more for others and celebrate their success!

I AM A LEADER!

_____
_____
_____
_____
_____
_____
_____
_____
_____
_____
_____
_____
_____

TODAY'S I-FFIRMATION

Day_____

I AM ENOUGH

I AM ENOUGH. I AM excited to be alive. I rejoice and re-choice every day to make my life better. I AM ENOUGH. I AM cool ENOUGH. Intelligent ENOUGH. Clever ENOUGH. I AM Capable ENOUGH. Imaginative ENOUGH. Talented ENOUGH. Poised ENOUGH. I have more than ENOUGH.

I AM ENOUGH!

_____
_____
_____
_____
_____
_____
_____
_____
_____
_____
_____
_____
_____
_____
_____
_____

TODAY'S I-FFIRMATION

Day_____

I AM A RISK TAKER

I trust my HEART. I believe in my DREAMS! I TRUST in GOD! I trust what I have learned and re-learned in my LIFE. I BELIEVE in my ability, talents, and skills. I Believe I AM more than CAPABLE. I AM A RISK TAKER. I AM taking calculated risks on a daily basis because I want to accomplish my DREAMS and GOALS! I AM willing to take a risk to achieve favorable results, even if they are small ones! I take risks even when I feel fear. I know my life is an experiment, so I can't ever get it wrong. I learn and grow from every experience. I AM A RISK TAKER. I do not fear taking a risk to welcome new people into my life! I AM willing to take risk to overcome my fear of rejection, fear of failure and fear of being alone on my journey! I trust in God's amazing grace.

I AM A RISK TAKER!

TODAY'S I-FFIRMATION

Day_____

I AM DILIGENT

I AM DILIGENT! I want to succeed, I will lookout for distractions. I have created a plan of action with a specific set of goals that I know will MAKE IT happen! I AM DILIGENT. I will continue to remove negative influences from my life; distractions such as food, people, activities and technology. I see opportunities for growth everywhere. I AM DILIGENT. Today and every day I choose to stay on task. I want to increase my faith and fulfill my mission to create success in my personal and professional life and this will always be central to me. I AM DILIGENT! I have to protect what I WANT and WHAT I NEED.

I AM DILIGENT!

TODAY'S I-FFIRMATION

Day_____

I AM SO DEEPLY GRATEFUL

I AM SO DEEPLY GRATEFUL because I AM blessed in so many ways. I AM SO DEEPLY GRATEFUL for my life, my family, my friends, my gifts and talents. I AM SO DEEPLY GRATEFUL for the flow of goodness and the blessings that are poured into all that I choose, create and do. The more GRATEFUL I AM, the more connected I AM to the source and power of creation. I AM SO DEEPLY GRATEFUL because I understand the source of abundance in my life. I AM SO DEEPLY GRATEFUL because I AM able to release all bitterness, resentment and dissatisfaction. In gratitude, I AM at peace with my life and able to remove myself from non-serving energies and focus wholly on creating amazing things and deeds that will bless others and me. With a grateful heart, I receive all the blessings coming my way. Today and every day.

I AM SO DEEPLY GRATEFUL!

_____
_____
_____
_____
_____
_____
_____

TODAY'S I-FFIRMATION

Day_____

I AM STILL

I AM STILL. Every breath I inhale calms me and every breath I exhale takes away tension and stress. Every cell in my body is relaxed and oozes with calmness. I AM STILL. I love myself deeply and unconditionally. I AM confident about solving life's problems successfully. I live in peace. I AM STILL. Everything is good in my world and I AM safe. My future is good. I look forward to the blessings in my life and their manifestation. I AM filled with hope and happiness. I AM STILL. Life is wonderful. I trust in God. I AM STILL. I AM surrounded by calm. The energy around is soothing.

I AM STILL!

TODAY'S I-FFIRMATION

Day_____

I AM CONFIDENT

I AM CONFIDENT, when I breathe; I inhale confidence and exhale nervousness. I love meeting strangers and approach them with boldness and enthusiasm. I accept myself and love myself deeply and completely. I AM CONFIDENT. I AM no longer held back by the negativity of my past or what others believe me to be. I AM CONFIDENT. I attract only the best of circumstances and the most positive people in my life. I AM CONFIDENT. I believe that God has given me special gifts, talents, and purpose to fulfill. I AM CONFIDENT. Each day I RISE to make a difference! Nothing is impossible and life is great.

I AM CONFIDENT!

_____
_____
_____
_____
_____
_____
_____
_____
_____
_____
_____
_____

TODAY'S I-FFIRMATION

Day_____

I AM CREATING

I AM CREATING. I AM the architect of my life. I AM the inventor of my reality. I accept and love myself just the way I AM. I AM CREATING. I AM supported and loved by the Creator. I AM CREATING. With a new enthusiastic approach, I AM creating new energy around me. I AM seeking out a new circle of influence. People who become my advocates and support my dreams and ideas. I AM able to achieve whatever I desire. I know I AM creating a new life. I AM creating a new me.

I AM CREATING!

_____
_____
_____
_____
_____
_____
_____
_____
_____
_____
_____
_____
_____
_____
_____
_____

TODAY'S I-FFIRMATION

Day_____

I AM HOPEFUL

I AM HOPEFUL! I AM HOPEFUL because it keeps me from surrendering to all that can take my focus off what really matters in my life. I AM HOPEFUL because my FAITH is the center of my being. I AM HOPEFUL. I expect great things to happen. There is always another way, new possibilities, opportunities, and blessings to celebrate. Because I AM HOPEFUL, I AM always headed in the right direction. I AM HOPEFUL for I AM surrounded by positive, healthy, and loving people. I AM HOPEFUL that all my desires will be fulfilled. I AM HOPEFUL for I rejoice in what I have and I know that fresh new experiences are ahead of me. There is always a better way. I CHOOSE HOPE!

I AM HOPEFUL!

_____
_____
_____
_____
_____
_____
_____
_____
_____
_____
_____

TODAY'S AFFIRMATION

Day _____

I AM TAKING ACTION EVERY DAY

Every positive action I take leads to greater success and gets me closer to my PURPOSE! Everything I do supports my desires for my future. I AM completely responsible for my actions. I AM TAKING ACTION. I act on every opportunity that comes my way. I AM always motivated. I AM always moving forward in my life. I AM TAKING ACTION when it comes to my purpose! I AM committed to putting 100% effort into my goals. I AM completely dedicated to doing everything it takes to reach my highest potential. I AM creating a great future for myself right now.

I AM TAKING ACTION!

_____
_____
_____
_____
_____
_____
_____
_____
_____
_____
_____
_____

TODAY'S I-FFIRMATION

Day_____

I AM SORTING

I AM SORTING to re-launch what I have to do to reach my PURPOSE! I AM SORTING and ready to eliminate items that are in my way. I AM SORTING through activities that are taking up my valuable time. I AM SORTING through the many things that I AM working on that seem to be important, and they really "are not." I AM SORTING through and re-focusing my time, efforts and resources on things that really matter…to me! Things that are in line with my values, my family, my faith, my business and my purpose! I AM SORTING. My steps have been ordered and I AM not wasting time!

I AM SORTING!

TODAY'S I-FFIRMATION

Day_____

I AM OUTSTANDING

I AM taking action. My journey has brought me to this point, shaken and reshaped by adversity and faith. I have learned much, seen more and suffered greatly. I AM taking action. My BREAKTHROUGH moment has arrived. I will no longer tell those STORIES of hurt, defeat, disappointment and brokenness. I AM Outstanding! I will Be OUTSTANDING! Speak Outstanding! Do Outstanding!

I AM OUTSTANDING!

_____
_____
_____
_____
_____
_____
_____
_____
_____
_____
_____
_____
_____
_____
_____

TODAY'S I-FFIRMATION

Day_____

I AM PREPARED

I AM PREPARED to do everything that I need to do to get into position for greatness. I know there is more out there for me. I know my BREAKTHROUGH is near. I AM PREPARED to receive all that is to come, because it is for me. I AM PREPARED to release the things that are holding me back such as; my limiting thoughts, situations, regrets and those things that have been keeping me back from my destiny. I AM PREPARED. I cannot redo or rewrite the chapters of my past, but I can change my present and future by re-learning and setting forth a new way of accomplishing things. I AM PREPARED and have a clear vision of hope for myself. I AM PREPARED to use my experiences, gifts and skills to secure my life's purpose. I AM PREPARED for all that is to come.

I AM PREPARED!

_____
_____
_____
_____
_____
_____
_____
_____
_____
_____
_____

TODAY'S AFFIRMATION

Day_____

I AM NOT A QUITTER

I AM NOT A QUITTER. On this day, I AM filled with determination and faith. I have been given a new day to create something new, fix something old and accept things as they are. I AM NOT A QUITTER because I AM motivated and on track to staying healthy, growing my business, and serving others. I know I can succeed and overcome my physical and mental obstacles as long as I don't give up. There is no time for complaining or judging. It is time to WORK and GET IT DONE! I AM NOT A QUITTER because my faith is strong. I AM NOT A QUITTER because I have purpose! I AM NOT A QUITTER because I AM committed to serving others and if I quit, I quit on them too. I AM NOT A QUITTER for as long as I have breath, I KNOW I CAN! And I Will!

I AM NOT A QUITTER!

_____
_____
_____
_____
_____
_____
_____
_____
_____
_____
_____

OUTRO

I am hopeful the last 30 days have elevated you to a place of POWER, that each i-ffirmation has strengthened you physically, mentally and emotionally. Most importantly, you are starting to see real changes in your results and desired outcomes. To expand on your personal POWER Ritual, if you feel comfortable, find someone to be accountable to. If you're only accountable to yourself, it's so easy to cheat yourself and make up excuses not to continue. Find a good friend to do this with, or work out a deal that you're going to e-mail or text message them daily letting them know whether or not you accomplished your daily i-ffirmation. If you miss a day, have a consequence to give them $5. This will create more leverage on you to actually follow through and DO IT.

Aside from a consequence to create leverage, also find a reward. How will you reward yourself after the 30 days? What will you do for yourself to really reinforce this new behavior?

The goal of our journey together has been to create a POWERFUL You. The POWER Ritual is something you can repeat over and over again. I am hopeful in a short amount of time; you will be the POWERFUL You that you desire to be.

#POWER ON!

REFERENCES

1. *"Forgive to Win!"* - Walter E. Jacobson, M.D. Psychiatrist, speaker and author

2. Personal SWOT Analysis by Mindtools
www.mindtools.com

3. *"Making the Most of Your Talents - Opportunities Self-Awareness and Personal Development"* - By Dr. Scott Williams, Department of Management, Raj Soin College of Business, Wright State University, Dayton, Ohio.

4. Power Mantra, "A 30-Day Guide to Your Power: Powerful Outcomes Through Powerful Words," Ivette Mayo, *Houston, Texas:* 2017

Made in the USA
Columbia, SC
06 June 2018